SALAMANDERS

by Edward J. Maruska

Content Adviser:
Winston Card,
Conservation Program
Manager, Cincinnati Zoo
& Botanical Garden

Published in the United States of America by The Child's World®
PO Box 326 • Chanhassen, MN 55317-0326
800-599-READ • www.childsworld.com

PHOTO CREDITS

© Chris Mattison/Frank Lane Picture Agency/Corbis: 6–7
© Daniel Borzynski/Alamy: 23 (bottom)
© David A. Northcott/Corbis: 4–5
© E. R. Degginger/Photo Researchers, Inc.: 24
© Gary Nafis: 26–27
© Gerold and Cynthia Merker/Visuals Unlimited: 14–15
© Jim McGuire: 16–17
© Joe McDonald/Corbis: 21
© Karl H. Switak/Photo Researchers, Inc.: 19
© Larry Minden/Minden Pictures: 13
© Lynda Richardson/Corbis: cover, 1, 8–9, 10–11
© WildPictures/Alamy: 23 (top)
© Zigmund Leszczynski/Animals Animals-Earth Scenes: 29

ACKNOWLEDGMENTS

The Child's World®: Mary Berendes, Publishing Director;
Katherine Stevenson, Editor

The Design Lab: Kathleen Petelinsek, Design and Page Production

LIBRARY OF CONGRESS CATALOGING-IN-PUBLICATION DATA

Maruska, Edward J.
  Salamanders / by Edward J. Maruska.
     p. cm. — (New naturebooks)
  Includes bibliographical references and index.
  ISBN 1-59296-648-9 (library bound : alk. paper)
  1. Salamanders—Juvenile literature. I. Title. II. Series.
  QL668.C2M27 2006
  597.8'5—dc22   2006001376

Table of Contents

On the cover: Spotted salamanders like this one are one of the most common salamanders in the United States. They grow to be about 7 inches (18 cm) long and get their name from their bright yellow spots.

Meet the Salamander!

Just outside of town is a quiet park with cool, shady woods and a small pond. A hiking trail wanders through the park, and you've walked along it more times than you can count. You've seen turtles and frogs and ducks and lots of other animals. But there's one animal you've walked right by without even knowing it was there! It's small and slippery, with spots on its skin, and it hides under logs and leaves, where you'd never think to look. What is this secretive creature? It's a salamander!

4

Eastern tiger salamanders belong to a group called "mole salamanders" (named because they dig under leaves and soil like moles to find bugs and other foods). Eastern tiger salamanders live mostly in the eastern and central U.S. and grow to be about 8 inches (20 cm) long.

What Are Salamanders?

Cold-blooded animals need outside heat to warm their bodies.

The salamander group includes newts, mud puppies, and sirens.

The earliest salamanders lived about 150 million years ago.

Salamanders are a kind of **amphibian**. Amphibians are cold-blooded animals that have backbones, as well as skin that is thin, moist, and hairless. Amphibians also have two stages to their lives. Most of them spend the first stage living in water. In their second (adult) stage, different kinds live either on land or in the water.

Amphibians are divided into three main groups. The first group is salamanders, which are amphibians with tails. There are about 360 different kinds, or **species**, of salamanders. The second group consists of frogs and toads, which are amphibians without tails. The third group is made up of some legless, wormlike creatures called *caecilians* (sih-SIL-yens).

This striped fire salamander lives in France. Fire salamanders are found in many parts of Europe.

What Do Salamanders Look Like?

At 14 inches (36 cm) long, the Pacific giant salamander is the biggest land-dwelling salamander in North America.

The smallest salamander of all lives in Mexico and has the scientific name *Thorius arboreus*. It measures only six-tenths of an inch (1.5 cm) from head to tail!

Salamanders have long, slim bodies and tails. They have flat heads with small eyes and wide mouths. They look a lot like lizards, but their skin is thinner and smoother than the tough, scaly skin of lizards.

Most salamanders aren't very big—6 inches (15 cm) or less in length. Some species, such as tiny pygmy salamanders, are less than two inches (5 cm) long. The largest salamander—in fact, the largest of all the amphibians—is the Japanese giant salamander, which can be over 5 feet (1.5 m) long!

8

Here you can see a marbled salamander resting on a fallen leaf in Virginia. These salamanders live mainly in the southeastern U.S. and grow to be about 4 inches (10 cm) long. They are named for the "marbled" look from the white and gray bands on their backs.

Most salamanders have four short legs, with four toes on each front foot and five toes on each back foot. Their legs are so short that their bellies drag on the ground when they walk. Like other amphibians, almost all salamanders lack claws. Salamanders use their long tails for balance if they are walking on land. They use them for swimming if they are in the water.

Most adult salamanders have lungs for breathing, but some have **gills**. Some "lungless salamanders" don't have either lungs or gills. Instead, they soak up oxygen only through their skin and the linings of their mouths and throats. They have to stay in wet places, because their skin can absorb oxygen only if it's wet.

Sirens are underwater salamanders that breathe through gills. They have no back legs, and they swim like fish, by waving their flat tails back and forth.

Most salamanders come in dark, dull colors that act as camouflage to help them hide. Some, however, have bright markings in red, orange, or yellow.

Mountain dusky salamanders like this one are lungless salamanders. They live in the eastern U.S. and are about 4 inches (10 cm) long. These salamanders have a stripe on their back that can be yellow, orange, green, gray, or even red. The stripe fades as they age, and older mountain duskies are often completely dark brown.

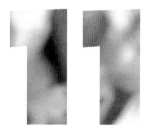

11

Where Do Salamanders Live?

Some salamanders can live in slightly salty water, but none can live in the ocean. Ocean water is too salty for their bodies.

Salamanders that live on land tend to be smaller. Those that live in the water tend to be bigger but have smaller legs.

Some salamanders that live in trees have a tail that can hold onto branches, like the tail of a monkey.

Salamanders live in many areas of the world, including North and Central America and the northern part of South America. Salamanders also live in Europe, the Near East, Africa, and Asia.

Some salamanders live only on land. Others live only in water. Still others, including all of the salamanders people called "newts," spend some of their time in the water and some of their time on land.

On land, salamanders tend to live in wooded, moist areas. They avoid the heat and sun by hiding in shallow **burrows**, in trees, or under rocks, logs, or fallen leaves.

12

This Pacific giant salamander is moving across a wet forest floor in California. These huge salamanders prefer to live near the fast-moving water of streams rather than the calm waters of ponds or lakes.

Most people aren't even aware of the salamanders that live in their area. Salamanders are usually **nocturnal**, or active mostly at night. They're also quiet and tend to live in dark, moist places where people seldom look.

Salamanders' skin is covered with a slimy coating of **mucus**. The mucus helps keep the skin from drying out if the animal is out of the water. It also helps the salamander absorb oxygen and keep the right balance of salt and water in its body.

Many salamanders live in areas that have mild summers but cold winters. When the weather gets too cold, these salamanders go into a deep sleep, or **hibernate**, until the weather warms up again.

Some sirens live in ponds or other water spots that dry up during the summer. They dig themselves into the muddy bottom. When the pond dries up, the siren's coating of mucus hardens. It can keep the animal from drying out for weeks.

You can really see the slime on this arboreal salamander's skin! These salamanders live in the western U.S. and grow to be about 4 inches (10 cm) long. Arboreal salamanders are terrific climbers—some have been found 60 feet (18 m) up in trees!

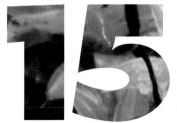

15

Some salamanders even live underground, in caves! Some of these cave salamanders live in the "twilight zone," where there is still some light from the entrance. Some, however, live farther back in the darkness. One region of Europe has an unusual cave salamander called an *olm*. Olms are a pale pink color. They live in underground streams and breathe through gills, although they also have lungs. Their eyes are so poorly developed that they can't see. Nevertheless, they can find food even in the darkness. They don't need much food, though! Amazingly, olms can go for several years without eating.

People used to think strange-looking olms like this one were baby dragons! Others called them "human fish" because they thought olms looked like a cross between a person and a fish.

Olms use their sense of smell to find food. Like sharks, they can also find food by sensing electricity in the water.

If olms grow up in darkness, they are a pale, pinkish white. If they are exposed to light, they turn darker, and their eyes develop somewhat. If they are put back in darkness, they lose their color again.

What Do Salamanders Eat?

Some kinds of land-dwelling salamanders have a long, sticky tongue for catching their prey.

Salamanders don't have ears. They can't hear higher sounds that move through the air, but they can feel lower sounds that travel through the water or the ground.

Salamanders are meat-eating **carnivores**. They are **predators** that hunt other animals for food—but usually not very quickly!

Those that live on land eat mostly small animals such as worms, slugs, and bugs. Sometimes they move up slowly on their **prey**, then grab it. Sometimes they sit and wait for their prey to come to them. Most land-dwelling salamanders do their hunting at night.

Salamanders that live in the water eat a variety of foods, including tadpoles, worms, fish eggs, bugs, and snails. Some types eat small fish, too. Water salamanders use their sense of smell to track down their prey. Then they open their mouths underwater and suck the prey inside.

This Pacific giant salamander is eating a banana slug in northern California.

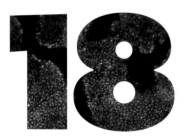

How Are Baby Salamanders Born?

Male salamanders sometimes show bright colors to attract females.

When a male smooth newt is looking for a mate, he grows a fin-like crest that runs along his entire back.

Some newts that lay eggs in shallow water carefully wrap each egg in leaves to protect it from sunlight and other dangers.

Salamanders hatch from eggs. Different kinds of salamanders lay their eggs in different places. Some lay them in water, and others lay them on land, perhaps in a log or other protected spot where the eggs will stay moist. Some salamanders lay their eggs one at a time, and others lay them in clumps—in some cases, over 400 eggs at a time. Salamanders that live in the water tend to lay more eggs at a time than those that spend some or all of their time on land.

Salamander eggs don't have any kind of eggshell to protect them. They're usually covered with a soft, jellylike material that keeps them moist. Some land-dwelling salamanders curl their bodies around their eggs and protect them until they hatch. One kind—the fire salamander— keeps its eggs inside its body until they hatch.

This adult Jefferson salamander is swimming near its eggs. These salamanders lay about 30 to 60 eggs at one time, and the eggs hatch in about two weeks. Jefferson salamanders live in the northeastern U.S. and southeastern Canada. They are named for Jefferson College in Pennsylvania.

What Are Baby Salamanders Like?

Some salamander larvae start out in the water, then live on land for a while, then return to the water as adults. When they are living on land, they are known as *efts*.

All salamanders start out the first stage of their lives as **larvae**. Salamander larvae have feathery gills on the outsides of their bodies for breathing underwater. Some land-dwelling species go through this larval stage while they are still inside their eggs. Fire salamanders go through this stage while they are still inside the mother's body. Still other species hatch from their eggs and actually live in the water during their larval stage.

The top picture shows a fire salamander larva as it swims in a pond. You can see the feathery gills on the sides of its head. The bottom picture shows a red eft—the larva of a red-spotted newt. When the eft reaches adulthood, it will return to the water and turn an olive or brownish green color.

After their larval stage, many salamanders go through a major change to become adults. Many species lose their gills and grow lungs for breathing. They also grow their adult legs and tongues. Some species, including mud puppies, only change partway from their larval form, keeping their gills and some other body parts.

As young salamanders get bigger, their front legs grow faster than their back legs. They also shed their old skin as they get bigger—and usually eat it.

The axolotl, which lives in Mexico, doesn't change out of its larval form in the wild. Scientists can make them change into adult salamanders by adding a certain substance to the water.

This adult mud puppy is swimming in a stream. You can see the red, feathery gills on the sides of its head. Mud puppies get their name because they are often seen crawling along the muddy bottoms of rivers and lakes.

How Do Salamanders Protect Themselves?

Salamanders don't make much noise, but if they are in danger, some kinds squeak or yelp.

Fire salamanders not only produce poison in their skin, they can squirt it at attackers.

When something threatens the California salamander, it stands tall by straightening its legs and raising its tail.

Some animals like to eat salamanders. They include skunks, raccoons, turtles, and birds. But salamanders have ways of protecting themselves, too. Many salamanders taste bad, and some even make a deadly poison in their skin. Poisonous salamanders often have bright colors—probably to warn their enemies away! Even poison doesn't stop some animals from eating salamanders, though.

Many salamanders can actually drop their tails if they get grabbed! They leave the wriggling tail behind and escape from their surprised enemy. Then they grow a new tail. In fact, salamanders can grow entire new legs, some parts of their hearts, and even parts of their eyes! Scientists are trying to learn how salamanders can grow so many new parts.

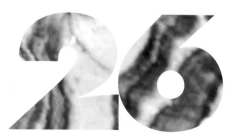

This arboreal salamander is missing the tip of its tail. It's not clear whether the salamander lost the tip in an accident or was attacked by an enemy. In time, however, the tip will grow back, as good as new.

Are Salamanders in Danger?

Hellbenders can live to be 25 years old in the wild. Some salamanders kept by people have lived to be older than 50!

Chinese giant salamanders are endangered, largely because the areas they live in are being destroyed. People also hunt them illegally for food and to use their body parts in medicines.

Scientists are worried about the future of many kinds of amphibians, including salamanders. Many salamander species are now **endangered**. As the number of people on our planet grows, large areas of forests are being cut down. Marshes, streams, and other places where salamanders live are being destroyed to make room for buildings, roads, and towns. Pollution is a problem, too, because salamanders' thin skin absorbs harmful pollutants easily. Diseases and global warming are other possible reasons why the number of amphibians is dropping.

We might not see wild salamanders very often, but they are amazing creatures and an important part of our natural world. Scientists are working hard to figure out why they and other amphibians are in danger—and what we can do about it.

Chinese giant salamanders are huge, growing up to 5 feet (1.5 m) long. They are very similar to Japanese giant salamanders, but Chinese giant salamanders have a longer tail and a pointier snout. Giant salamanders are so large, when the first fossil was discovered in 1726, scientists thought they were looking at the bones of a person!

Glossary

amphibian (am-FIH-bee-un) Amphibians are animals that have backbones and moist, smooth skin and need outside heat to warm their bodies. Salamanders are amphibians.

burrows (BUR-ohz) Burrows are underground holes animals dig or use as their homes. Salamanders sometimes hide in burrows.

camouflage (KA-muh-flazh) Camouflage is special coloring or markings that help an animal blend in with its surroundings. Most salamanders have camouflage.

carnivores (KAR-nuh-vorz) Carnivores are meat-eating animals. Salamanders are carnivores.

endangered (in-DAYN-jurd) An endangered animal is one that is close to dying out. Many species of salamanders are endangered.

gills (GILZ) Gills are organs on some animals that allow the animals to breathe underwater. Some adult salamanders have gills.

hibernate (HY-bur-nayt) To hibernate is to go into a very deep sleep, to save energy and survive through the winter. Salamanders in colder areas hibernate until warmer weather arrives.

larvae (LAR-vee) In some animals, a larva is the young, very different form of the animal when it first hatches or is born. The larva goes through big changes before it becomes an adult.

mucus (MYOO-kuss) Mucus is a wet slime produced by some animals' bodies. Salamanders are covered with mucus.

nocturnal (nok-TUR-nul) An animal that is nocturnal is active mostly at night and rests during the day. Most salamanders are nocturnal.

predators (PREH-duh-terz) Predators are animals that hunt and kill other animals for food. Salamanders are predators.

prey (PRAY) Prey are animals that other animals hunt as food. Worms, slugs, and bugs are common prey for salamanders.

species (SPEE-sheez) An animal species is a group of animals that share the same features and can have babies only with animals in the same group. There are about 360 different species of salamanders.

To Find Out More

Read It!

Bernhard, Emery, and Durga Bernhard (illustrator). *Salamanders.* New York: Holiday House, 1995.

Himmelman, John. *A Salamander's Life.* Danbury, CT: Children's Press, 1998.

Johnston, Ginny, and Judy Cutchins. *Slippery Babies: Young Frogs, Toads, and Salamanders.* New York: Morrow Junior Books, 1991.

Miller, Sara Swan. *Salamanders: Secret, Silent Lives.* Danbury, CT: Franklin Watts, 2000.

Parker, Nancy Winslow, and Joan Richards Wright (illustrator). *Frogs, Toads, and Salamanders.* New York: Greenwillow Books, 1990.

Winner, Cherie. *Salamanders.* Minneapolis, MN: Carolrhoda Books, 1993.

On the Web

Visit our home page for lots of links about salamanders: *http://www.childsworld.com/links*

Note to Parents, Teachers, and Librarians: We routinely check our Web links to make sure they're safe, active sites—so encourage your readers to check them out!

31

Index

About the Author

Edward J. Maruska has authored more than 20 books and articles on salamanders, amphibians, and natural history. His zoo experience began in 1956 when he was hired by Marlin Perkins to work as a zookeeper at the Lincoln Park Zoo in Chicago. Mr. Maruska became the Director of the Cincinnati Zoo and Botanical Garden in 1968 and served as its director for 32 years before retiring in 2000. Edward grew up in Illinois and Wisconsin, where he became interested in amphibians by haunting the breeding ponds of frogs and salamanders near his home.